Bookworms

Migrating Animals

Geese

B.J. Best

Cavendish Square
New York

Published in 2017 by Cavendish Square Publishing, LLC
243 5th Avenue, Suite 136, New York, NY 10016

First Edition

Library of Congress Cataloging-in-Publication Data

Names: Best, B.J.
Title: Geese / B.J. Best.
Description: New York : Cavendish Square, 2017. | Series: Migrating animals | Includes index.
Identifiers: ISBN 9781502620989 (pbk.) | ISBN 9781502621009 (library bound) | ISBN 9781502620996 (6 pack) | ISBN 9781502621016 (ebook)
Subjects: LCSH: Geese--Juvenile literature.
Classification: LCC QL696.A52 B4475 2017 | DDC 598.4'17--dc23

Editorial Director: David McNamara
Copy Editor: Nathan Heidelberger
Associate Art Director: Amy Greenan
Designer: Alan Sliwinski
Production Coordinator: Karol Szymczuk
Photo Research: J8 Media

The photographs in this book are used by permission and through the courtesy of: Cover WayneDuguay/Shutterstock.com; p. 5 Karel Bartik/Shutterstock.com; p. 7 sevenke/Shutterstock.com; p. 9 Brian Guest/Shutterstock.com; pp.11, 13 Sergey Gorshkov/Minden Pictures/Getty Images; p. 15 Olivier Juneau/Shutterstock.com; p. 17 VisionsofAmerica/Joe Sohm/Getty Images; p. 19 Raul Touzon/Getty Images; p. 21 James L. Amos/Getty Images.

Printed in the United States of America

Contents

Geese live all around the world.

They are water birds.

Most geese **migrate**.

They fly north in the spring.

They fly south in the fall.

Geese fly in a V shape.

It helps geese save energy.

Snow geese spend summers in **Canada**.

They live on the **tundra**.

In Canada, snow geese
have chicks.

They are known as **goslings**.

In autumn it gets cold.

The snow geese fly south
in large groups.

They need food.

The geese travel on **flyways**.

Flyways are like roads in the sky.

Snow geese can fly about 3,000 miles (4,800 kilometers)!

Snow geese spend winter in the South.

It is warm there.

In spring, the geese fly north.

They return to Canada.

Soon there will be
new goslings!

New Words

Canada (CAN-uh-duh) The country north of the United States.

flyways (FLY-ways) Paths in the air for migrating birds.

goslings (GAHZ-lings) Baby geese.

migrate (MY-grate) To travel far to live in a new place.

tundra (TUN-druh) A cold, large land area.

Index

About the Author

B.J. Best lives in Wisconsin with his wife and son. He has written several other books for children. He sees geese migrate every fall.

About BOOKWORMS

Bookworms help independent readers gain reading confidence through high-frequency words, simple sentences, and strong picture/text support. Each book explores a concept that helps children relate what they read to the world they live in.